Common Ground in Electronically Mediated Conversation

Synthesis Lectures on Human-Centered Informatics

Editor

John M. Carroll, *Edward M. Frymoyer Professor of Information Sciences and Technology, Penn State University*

Common Ground in Electronically Mediated Conversation
Andrew Monk

ISBN: 978-3-031-01056-9   print
ISBN: 978-3-031-02184-8   ebook

DOI: 10.1007/978-3-031-02184-8

A Publication in the Springer series

SYNTHESIS LECTURES ON HUMAN-CENTERED INFORMATICS # 1
Lecture #1

Series Editor: John M. Carroll, Penn State University

Common Ground in Electronically Mediated Conversation

Andrew Monk
University of York

SYNTHESIS LECTURES ON HUMAN–CENTERED INFORMATICS # 1

ABSTRACT

Technologies that electronically mediate conversation, such as text-based chat or desktop video conferencing, draw on theories of human–human interaction to make predictions about the effects of design decisions. This lecture reviews the theory that has been most influential in this area: Clark's theory of language use. The key concept in Clark's theory is that of common ground. Language is viewed as a collaborative activity that uses existing common ground to develop further common ground and, hence, to communicate efficiently. The theory (a) defines different kinds of common ground, (b) formalizes the notion of collaborative activity as a "joint action," and (c) describes the processes by which common ground is developed through joint action. Chapter 1 explains why a purely cognitive model of communication is not enough and what is meant by the phrase "collaborative activity." Chapter 2 introduces the idea of common ground and how it is used in language through an example of two people conversing over a video link. Chapter 3 indicates where the interested reader can find out about the antecedents to Clark's theory. Chapter 4 sets out the fundamental concepts in Clark's theory. Chapter 5 uses five published case studies of electronically mediated communication to illustrate the value of the theory. These include studies of a computer-supported meeting room (Cognoter), a video tunnel that supports gaze awareness, video conferencing in medical consultation, and text chat.

KEYWORDS

Herbert Clark, common ground, mediated communication, language use, theory, video, communication, text chat

Preface

Human-centered informatics (HCI) started as the study of an individual interacting with a computer. Very quickly, it became clear that digital devices have enormous potential for communication and the discipline moved on to encompass technologies that electronically mediate human–human interaction, such as text-based chat or video conferencing. The designers of such facilities need answers to questions that depend on a knowledge of how we use language. What communication tasks will benefit from a shared whiteboard? When are text messages better than speech? The theory that informs the design of these artifacts is a theory of human–human interaction (i.e., language use).

Previous theories of language use are divided into the cognitive and the social. Most psycholinguistic accounts of language production and comprehension are very cognitive. They are solely concerned with an individual's behavior and the information processing going on in that individual's head. Ethnomethodological and other sociological accounts of language use are, in contrast, social. They concentrate on the structure that is observable in the behavior of groups. Herbert Clark has developed a theory of language use that bridges these two camps. In Clark's theory, individuals have their own individual goals and behavior but also collaborate in such a way that something more emerges when one considers them as a group. To make this step from the individual to the social, the theory defines the notion of a collaborative activity and outlines the processes needed for a collaborative activity to succeed. Most importantly for HCI researchers, this theory has been found to be useful in the sense that it can make practically relevant predictions for the design of facilities to electronically mediate conversation.

The key concept in Clark's theory is that of common ground. Language is viewed as a collaborative activity that uses existing common ground to develop further common ground and, hence, to communicate efficiently. The lecture starts by explaining why an individual cognitive model of communication is not enough and what is meant by the phrase "collaborative activity." It then introduces the idea of common ground and how it is used in language through an example of two people communicating over a video link. Chapter 4 sets out the fundamental concepts in Clark's theory in some detail. Chapter 5 uses five published case studies of mediated communication to illustrate the value of the theory. These include studies of a computer-supported meeting room, a video tunnel that supports gaze awareness, video conferencing in medical consultation, and text chat.

The lecture is intended for use by readers unfamiliar with theories of language use who wish to find out more about Clark's theory and the work that has been done applying it to the design of electronically mediated communication. It can be approached from two viewpoints. Some readers will be mainly concerned with the design of facilities for electronically mediated communication using video, speech, or text. These readers will be interested in the possibilities offered by the theory for suggesting how such systems should be designed. Other readers may be interested in the insights that the study of electronically mediated communication can provide to our understanding of conversation in general. For this reason, the lecture may be used by students and researchers coming from an electronic design background or from a more linguistic background.

Contents

CHAPTER 1

Motivation—Conversation as a Collaborative Activity

As well as how individuals interact with computers, research in human-centered informatics (HCI) includes the study of electronic devices for the purpose of communication, for example, video conferencing systems, text-based chat, and e-mail. Some of the questions designers need to answer about these systems have to do with an individual interacting with the device, for example, how to use the limited display on a mobile phone, but others have to do with the way that we use language, for example, what communication tasks will benefit from a shared whiteboard. The theory that answers these latter questions is a theory of human-human communication. This lecture is concerned with one such theory: Clark's theory of common ground.

1.1 PRODUCTION + COMPREHENSION ≠ COMMUNICATION

One view of human-human communication conceptualizes language as a sender producing some utterance that is then comprehended by a receiver. While this has value, it is not the whole story.

The upper part of Figure 1 depicts a much-simplified model of how two computers communicate with one another. Computer A sends the sequence of characters forming an e-mail message by looking up a digital code for each letter. Each digital code is then translated into a pattern of voltage changes on a wire. Computer B reverses this process. It registers the pattern of voltage changes, converts this into a digital code, and looks up the letter. When enough letters have been accumulated, it can display the e-mail. This conception of information transmission was used by Shannon & Weaver (1949) to formulate a mathematical theory of communication that has been used by communication engineers for many years.

The lower part of Figure 1 takes the information transmission model as an analogy for human-human communication. Some representation of the meaning of a word in person A's head is looked up to find its phonemic representation, and that is then converted to sound pressure changes

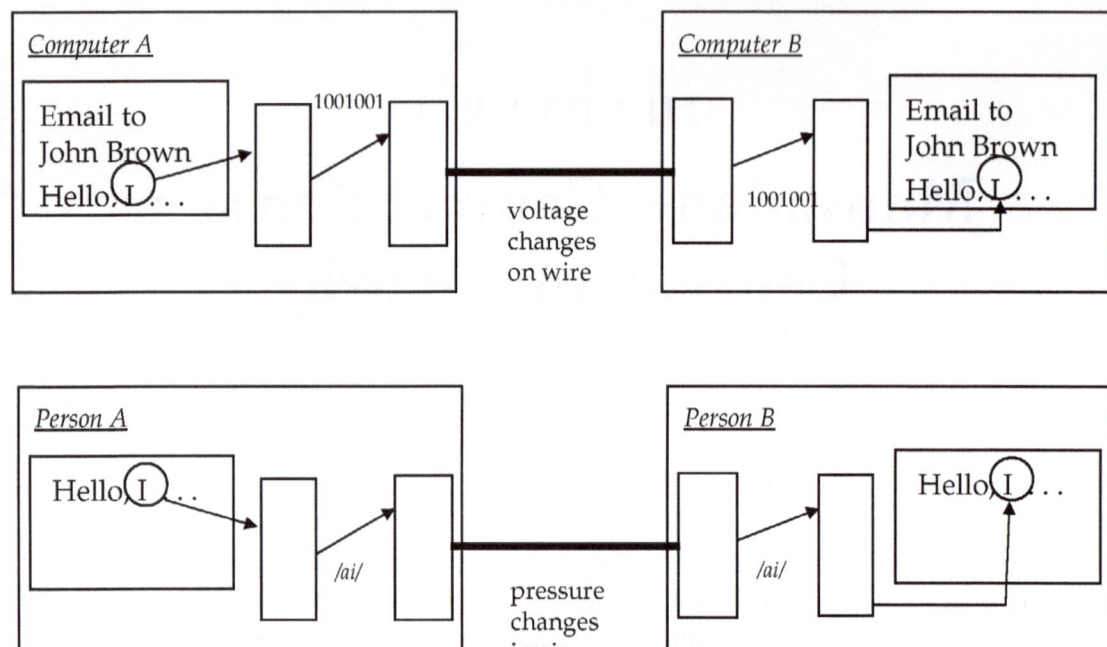

FIGURE 1: The information transfer model of communication; top panel, as applied to communicating computers; bottom panel, as the encoding-decoding model of human-human communication.

in the air by person A's vocal apparatus. Person B's ear registers these pressure changes and auditory processing in B's brain converts them to a phonemic representation and then to a representation of the meaning of the word.

This information-processing model allows one to decompose the process of communication into two parts: speech production and speech comprehension. Speech production is the process of converting meaning to sound pressure changes and speech comprehension is the process of converting speech pressure changes back into meaning. Figure 1 is a very simplified version of current understanding. The linguists, psycholinguists, and speech scientists who study what goes on within each of these two processes have developed sophisticated models hypothesizing many different representations that may be generated along the way (see, e.g., Altmann, 1997).

The models developed have resulted in many practical advances. Research on speech comprehension has led to improvements in digital hearing aids and speech recognition software. The research on speech production has led to speech synthesis software and speech therapy programs for stroke victims. This approach to language use has, however, proved less useful in providing guidelines for the design and configuration of electronic communication systems. For example, if one is designing a video conferencing configuration, should one use the camera to convey as much information as possible about detailed facial expression and lip movements of the person currently talking, or would it be more valuable to provide a wide-angle view of what everyone at the other end is doing? When does text have advantages over speech?

The problem is that models of speech production and speech comprehension are cognitive models. They are models of what goes on in an individual's head. It turns out that, to answer the questions posed above, we need a social model (i.e., a model of how a pair or group of individuals use language as an ensemble). It is not intuitively obvious why this should be so. Common sense says that, if we have a model of how a speaker produces speech and another of how a listener

TABLE 1: A snippet of real conversation (Jefferson, 1987)	
Roger:	Did you have oil in it
Al:	Yeah, I-I mean I changed the oil, put new oil filters, r- completely redid the oil system, had to put new gaskets on the oil pan to stop-stop the leak, and then I put -and then-
Roger:	That was a gas leak
Al:	It was an oil leak buddy
Roger:	It's a gas leak
Al:	It's an oil ⌐ leak!
Roger:	⌐ on the number one jug
Al:	It's an oil leak!
Roger:	Outta where, the pan?
Al:	Yeah
Roger:	Oh you put a new gasket on it stopped leaking
Al:	Uh huh

comprehends it, then it should be possible to simply put them together to form a model of language use. Section 1.2 explains why we need something more.

1.2   COLLABORATION IN LANGUAGE USE

Consider the conversation recorded in Table 1. Al has been mending Roger's car. Roger comes to the conversation thinking that the problem involved a petrol ("gas") leak. Al has just fixed an oil leak. What follows is a process of realignment. This language process is described as "repair." It starts when Roger senses "trouble" in the conversation because Al is talking about fixing the oil system. He signals this to Al with the utterance "that was a gas leak." They then collaborate until conversational repair is achieved. Eventually, Roger signals that he now sees there was an oil leak by saying "outta where, the pan?," the pan being the oil sump. Al then signals that he understands that Roger now understands this with his utterance "Yeah."

This is very different from the picture of communication presented in Figure 1. First of all, notice how ill formed and imprecise the utterances are with repetitions and restarts (e.g., "r-completely re-did"). There is also overlapping speech. The tabulation in Table 1 shows that "leak!" and "on the number one jug" were overlapping in time. Al and Roger get away with this imprecision because communication is a collaborative activity not just a matter of using a well-defined code to replicate the contents of one person's head in another's.

Al and Roger come to the conversation with different assumptions and priorities. They go away with different assumptions and priorities but they have developed sufficient common ground to serve each of their separate purposes. The conversation is a collaborative process in which they each endeavor to communicate sufficiently for their own purposes. At the same time, they monitor the conversation for evidence that the other person is or is not communicating sufficiently well for their purposes. Thus, each of them has an obligation to signal to the other when they sense communication is failing. Each of them has an obligation to monitor the conversation for such signals and to take appropriate actions to repair the situation until the other signals all is now well. This mutual pact is the basis of every conversation.

We can now see what the information transfer model depicted in Figure 1 is lacking. Communicating computers have a common code. This is possible because the code is well defined and can be programmed into both computers by engineers. In contrast, everyday spoken language is very ambiguous and only works because the parties actively collaborate to make it do so. Experience may have programmed you and I with the same rules for converting sounds into phonemes and for combining phonemes into words. However, when it comes to communicating intent or history, I cannot just look up a recipe that will copy what is in my head into yours, nor would I want to. Spoken language use is efficient precisely because only the information relevant to each individual's separate needs is communicated.

The above is the starting point for the collaborative model of conversation assumed by Herbert Clark. The remainder of this lecture describes his theory in more detail and illustrates how it can be used to explain various observations about electronically mediated human-human communication.

. . . .

CHAPTER 2

Overview—Developing Common Ground, An Example

This chapter introduces the notion of common ground and how it is used in language. Chapter 4 contains a more detailed treatment of the other fundamental concepts in Clark's theory.

Clark's theory is based around the concept of common ground, that is, the things we know about what is known by the person we are talking to. If this seems rather recursive, that is because it is. Clark's definition[1] of common ground implies that:

> a proposition p is only common ground if all the people conversing know p and they all know that they all know p.

This definition of common ground allows one to move between a view of language as an activity carried out by an ensemble of people (the social viewpoint) and a view of language as an activity carried out by individuals (the cognitive approach). The social viewpoint is developed by providing a detailed description of the activity by which the ensemble of conversants use and increase common ground. The cognitive viewpoint is developed by describing how an individual comes to know what is known by the others.

The nature of common ground is best explained by an example. This example will also illustrate how Clark's theory can help us understand the way that technology may affect the process

---

[1]Clark's formal definition of common ground is as follows:

p is common ground for members of C if and only if:

i. the members of C have information that p and that i.

This implies:

everyone in C knows p,

everyone in C knows everyone in C knows p,

everyone in C knows everyone in C knows everyone in C knows p,

and so on.

of communication. Consider two people using a desktop video conferencing package to discuss an architectural plan. They are wearing headphones with boom microphones and each can hear what the other says without difficulty. Each can view changes in the other person's facial expression via a head-and-shoulders view in a small video window. The remainder of the screen is taken up with a shared view of the architectural plan. Let us say that they have never met before. Even so, they can make some assumptions about common ground. First, there will be some common task defined by the work context. Let us say that Anne is an architect and Ben is someone who has hired Anne to design a house for him. The common task, negotiated in their previous correspondence, is to agree what small changes need to be made to make the plan final. They also know they have the common ground that comes from living in the same town.

They can assume certain conventions with respect to the communication process. They will speak English. They will both try to use language that the other will understand and to monitor the conversation for potential misunderstandings. When one feels that he/she does not understand something sufficiently for his/her current purpose, that person will signal this to the other person.

From the video images, they can make assumptions about their respective ages and genders that may have a bearing on how they express themselves. Also, Anne will assume that Ben will not have the same detailed knowledge of architectural terms that she has. As the conversation develops, she modifies this opinion. Ben uses the term "architrave" correctly so she tries more technical (and, hence, more concise) terms in her utterances. These do not cause trouble in the conversation so she continues to use them. Later, however, Ben does not understand the term "lintel." Anne picks this up from his facial expression and explains it to him. During this explanation, Ben demonstrates his understanding and they now both assume that this is common ground.

Ben describes how he would like the door of one bedroom, the one that faces south, to move. The architectural drawing is larger than the screen, and so this bedroom can only be seen by scrolling from the initial view. In their discussion of a previous detail, Ben has scrolled to this view but Ann has not. He has no way of knowing this. Everyday experience leads him to assume the general principle that what he can see she can see also. This false assumption of common ground causes problems when he uses the phrase "up there on the left." After some time, they realize they are talking at cross purposes and go about repairing their common ground.

At the end of the meeting, they check their common ground regarding the original work objective and agree that the drawing can be sent to the builder. As this has legal implications, Anne suggests that she sends Ben a paper copy of the modified plan and Ben agrees to formally accept the plan in a letter. This change of communication medium permits rereading so that each party can ensure that they really have achieved common ground.

The scenario sketched above illustrates the way common ground is used and how technology can affect the process of developing it. Table 2 summarizes some of the common ground exem-

TABLE 2: Some of the common ground used and developed (see text for explanation)
Conversational conventions
We will each try to be as concise as possible but take account of the background of the other person.
We will each make it clear to the other person when we cannot understand something sufficiently for our (individual) current purpose.
Communal common ground
We will speak in English.
We are both professional people.
We both live in the same town.
Personal common ground achieved before the conversation
Our joint purpose is to sign off the plan.
Personal common ground developed during the conversation
The door on the bedroom that faces south has to be moved.
When we use the term "lintel," we mean the horizontal supporting beam above a door or window.
We can both (now) see the bedroom that faces south on the plan.
The plan can go to the builder.

plified there under three categories: conversational conventions, communal common ground, and personal common ground.

Conversational conventions are the assumptions Clark states we must make to converse at all. The two examples given here are not meant to be exhaustive or well defined; Clark takes a whole book to do this! Knowing what communities a person belongs to allows us to make certain assumptions about existing common ground. Communal common ground is common ground that can be assumed from our experience of these different communities. Personal common ground is the common ground personal to the particular conversants under consideration, that is, the common ground assumed from our experience with the other individual.

By describing language use in this way, we can begin to understand how the technology impinges on the conversation in the way that it does. If Ann had not been able to detect Ben's puzzlement because there was no video image of his face, then Ben would have had to have signaled it in what he said. In some circumstances, Ben might have been loath to do this and a serious conversational breakdown could have occurred. The false assumption of common ground made by Ben could have been avoided if scrolling on his machine automatically resulted in scrolling on Ann's (so-called linked scrolling). We can also see why some media are better than others in certain circumstances.

This chapter has explained what common ground is as an introduction to Clark's theory. Clark's theory explains the process by which common ground is used and developed in conversation. This, the main part of the theory, is outlined in Chapter 4.

·   ·   ·   ·

CHAPTER 3

Scientific Foundations

Questions concerning the interpretation of language are not new and have been explored by philosophers of language for centuries. In the late 1600s, John Locke, for instance, attempted to conceptualize at an abstract level how simple and complex words are used and interpreted. But it is only relatively recently that social scientists have conducted empirical studies of language use. Technological developments such as audio and video recorders meant that talk as opposed to text could be documented and analyzed at a level of detail not before possible.

In the late 1970s, sociologists such as Garfinkel, Sacks, and Goffman turned their attention to the everyday and the taken-for-granted. As techniques such as discourse analysis developed, it became possible to identify ethnomethods; the taken-for-granted means of accomplishing interaction. In-depth qualitative analyses uncovered previously overlooked phenomena such as turntaking, the process by which we signal that we are about to respond or we wish our interlocutor to respond.

The view of language use as simple information transfer corresponds to many people's common sense view of what is going on, and so, it has taken many years for this alternative notion of language use as a collaborative activity to gain popularity. As indicated above, the prime movers in this shift have been social scientists. Ethnomethodologists such as Goffman (1976) and Sacks et al. (1974) have been very influential, as have philosophers such as Grice (1957). As social scientists, these authors take an approach that is at odds with the cognitive approach that is more commonly adopted by psychologists. For example, sociological accounts generally avoid attributing intentions to individuals, whereas intention is the basis of more cognitive accounts (Monk, 1998). What Clark has achieved is a marrying of these two approaches through his concept of a "joint action" (see below).

Readers with an interest in the building blocks of his approach can consult the following. McCarthy & Monk (1994) is a longer tutorial paper along the lines of Chapter 1. Clark's book (1996) is a coherent statement of his whole theory that cites many references to the social science it is based on. There are also the original papers cited in these two sources.

· · · ·

CHAPTER 4

The Theory in More Detail

Chapter 2 defined different kinds of common ground and informally described some of the mechanisms by which common ground is developed through an example. This chapter develops these ideas through some more formally defined concepts. The first part of the chapter sets out the fundamental assumptions made by Clark. First, he argues that face-to-face communication, rather than written language, should be the basis of a theory of language. He then points out, and defines for his own purposes, some known properties of face-to-face communication, that it involves more than just words, is a joint action, minimizes effort, and develops common ground. The second part of this chapter outlines some concepts that build on these fundamentals. These are the process of grounding, levels of collaborative activity, layers, and tracks.

4.1 FUNDAMENTALS

4.1.1 Face-to-Face Conversation is "Basic"

Much work in linguistics starts from an analysis of well-formed written text. Clark argues that real spoken conversations are a better starting point, even if they are messier. Children appear to learn how to do face-to-face communication spontaneously. Learning to read and write requires formal instruction. Indeed, a large part of the population of the world only has spoken language. If face-to-face speech is the basis of all our language behavior, then our understanding of other ways of communication should build on our understanding of face-to-face communication, not the other way around.

4.1.2 Face-to-Face Conversation Involves More Than Just Words

One of the major contributions of ethnomethodologists such as the conversational analysts (see, e.g., Sacks et al., 1974) has been to describe in detail how we use hands, face, eyes, and body in combination with the world we are in to facilitate the conversation. As well as the various cues used to manage turn taking, these "instruments" can be used to signal meaning to someone else. Table 3 is adapted from Clark (1996) and lists examples of how we do this. Normally, we think of language just as a process of describing things using words (i.e., the table cell in italics), but we sometimes

TABLE 3: Methods of signaling			
INSTRUMENT	DESCRIBING-AS	INDICATING	DEMONSTRATING
Voice	*Words, sentences*	"I," "here"	Tone of voice
Hands, arms	Emblems	Pointing	Iconic gestures
Face	Facial emblems	Pointing	Smiles
Eyes	Winking	Eye gaze	Smiles
Body	Junctions	Pointing	Iconic gestures

The voice is not the only instrument for communication in a face-to-face conversation. Adapted from Clark (1996, p. 188)

describe things with our hands. We might describe the shape of something by making our hands into that shape. Pointing is another important signal in language use. Pointing saves a lot of words and can be done by voice (e.g., "that there"), with a finger, or even with the eyes and face. Clark's final category of signal is demonstrating. We can demonstrate a gesture or tone of voice by imitating it. Clark suggests that a smile is best thought of as a signal to demonstrates one's happiness to someone else.

4.1.3   Face-to-Face Conversation is a Joint Action

As explained above, it does not make sense to think of language use except as a joint action involving two or more people. As such, it presents the same problems as any other joint action, such as playing a duet or shaking hands. In particular, there is a need for "coordinating devices," such as conventions or jointly salient perceptual events that are part of common ground. Clark uses this observation to explain many of the more detailed characteristics of language use described in the book. The key characteristics of a joint action are that both people involved intend to do their part and believe that the joint action includes their part and the other's. He uses a recursive definition of joint action.[1]

Ensemble A and B is doing joint action *k* if and only if:

0.   The action k includes 1. and 2.
1.   A intends to be doing A's part of k and believes 0.
2.   B intends to be doing B's part of k and believes 0.

[1] I am aware that some readers of this lecture may not find these quasi-mathematical formalisms as useful as I do. If you are such a reader, you should be able to follow the argument from the text surrounding them alone.

This definition, which applies to all joint actions, including language, implies:

A believes *k* includes A's part plus B's part,

A intends to do A's part,

B believes A intends to do A's part,

A believes B believes A intends to do A's part,

and so on.

4.1.4   Face-to-Face Conversation Uses Common Ground to Minimize the Effort Required to Communicate

As should be apparent by now, the key concept in Clark's theory is common ground.

> Everything we do is rooted in information we have about our surroundings, activities, percep-
> tions, emotions, plans, interests. Everything we do jointly with others is also rooted in this
> information, but only in that part we think they share with us.
> Clark & Brennan (1991, p. 92).

As was pointed out in Chapter 2, we make our assumptions about common ground on various bases. Some are to do with the groups we belong to. Very soon after meeting you, I will be able to make assumptions about the extent and detail of our common ground coming from our languages, nationalities, genders, ages, and occupations. Other bases for making assumptions about common ground depend on our history together.

By making assumptions of common ground, face-to-face conversation becomes extremely efficient. Even a grunt can communicate meaning in a context that is well understood by both conversants. This extreme efficiency is only possible because the joint action of language includes an intention to communicate efficiently. I must be able to assume that you are intending that I should understand what you are saying. Further, I must be able to assume that you are intending to do this in the most efficient way possible; otherwise, ambiguities will arise. This notion of efficiency was reformulated by (Clark & Brennan, 1991) as a matter of minimizing communication costs and then used to predict the effects of different ways of mediating communication (see Section 5.1).

4.1.5   Face-to-Face Conversation Develops Common Ground

The effect of conversation is to test, reformulate, and add to our common ground, and so, the most important source of common ground is our history of joint actions together.

One example of this personal common ground is the private lexicons of words that lovers develop together. Another more mundane example is the use of whiteboards or flip charts in meetings to form easily accessed references to previously established common ground. Thus, someone can point at a somewhat cryptic heading on a whiteboard and in a single gesture refer to the common ground that may have taken several minutes to establish in the first place. So economical and effective is this form of common ground that people talking in the corridor have been known to construct imaginary "air whiteboards" that they can point to later in the conversation.

4.2 GROUNDING, LEVELS, LAYERS, AND TRACKS

The previous section presented the concepts that Clark's theory is based on. Before going on to describe how these concepts relate to studies of electronically mediated communication, four further constructs need to be explained. They are the process of grounding, levels of joint action, layers, and tracks.

Figure 2 depicts the microstructure of the process that Clark describes as "grounding" (i.e., the process of developing common ground).

1. Anne presents an utterance u for Ben to consider. Anne takes account of the common ground that already exists between them to present u in a form she believes Ben will understand. Ben attempts to infer the import of u, interpreting it as u'.
2. Ben provides some evidence e that, from his point of view, all is well with the conversation. This might be simply to continue with the next turn in a sensible way. Alternatively, Ben might rephrase the utterance and play it back to Anne. Anne interprets e as e'. On the basis

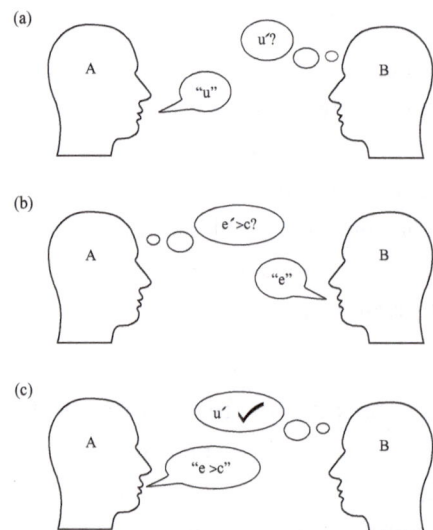

FIGURE 2: Clark's grounding process. u = utterance, u' = understanding of utterance, e = evidence of understanding sufficient for current purposes, e' = understanding of evidence of..., c = grounding criterion.

of e' and the common ground they have already developed, Anne then has to make a judgment whether or not Ben has understood u "sufficient for current purposes."

3. Finally, Anne signals to Ben that she understands that he has an understanding sufficient for current purposes. Again, this is most commonly done by simply continuing with some relevant next utterance. Necessary words like "yeah" or "uhuh" can also serve this purpose. If she is not satisfied that e' meets the grounding criteria, she can query e or re-present u.

This notion of a closely coupled grounding process is used in Section 5.2 to explain the problems observed with a Computer Supported Cooperative Work (CSCW) system.

The process of grounding described above elaborates the sequence in which common ground is observed in the structure of face-to-face conversation. The notion of levels of shared action further elaborates the process by describing the joint actions that all have to be in place for this process to work.

Table 4 lists the four levels of shared action that Clark suggests are necessary for effective conversation. They can be thought of as an "action ladder" to be read from the bottom. So the first requisite is that A and B have joint action 1. Refer back to the definition of a joint action in Section 4.1. Joint action 1 has two parts, one for A (behaving for B) and one for B (attending to A). The definition of a joint action implies that they are both intending to take these parts and believe that the other is doing likewise. Joint action 2 is for A to present signals to B and B to identify them. Joint action 2 depends on joint action 1 happening simultaneously. If B is not attending, then she cannot identify the signal. Clark describes this as the principle of upward completion. Joint action 3, which depends on and happens simultaneously with joint actions 1 and 2, is where A signals some proposition and B recognizes that A means that proposition. Finally, joint action 4 is where A proposes a joint project and B considers it.

	SPEAKER A'S PART	ADDRESSEE B'S PART
4	A is proposing a joint project w to B	B is considering A's proposal of w
3	A is signaling that p for B	B is recognizing that p from A
2	A is presenting signal s to	B is identifying signal s from A
1	A is executing behavior t for B	B is attending to behavior t from A

TABLE 4: The action ladder: levels of simultaneous joint action needed to converse

The example Clark uses to illustrate this is an occasion when he bought something in a drug store. Clark walks up to the counter, where the assistant is busy checking stock. The assistant says "I'll be there." At level 1, Clark and the assistant have engaged on a joint action where the assistant says something and knows that Clark will listen. At level 2, they are similarly engaged in a joint action where the assistant utters the words "I'll," "be," and "there," knowing that Clark will identify them. At level 3, the assistant knows that Clark is engaged in recognizing this signal as a proposition. Of course, what the assistant was really doing was the level 4 joint action of proposing a joint project. Clark's part in this joint proposal is to wait, the assistant's part is to finish what he or she is doing. The notion of levels of joint action is used in Section 5.3 to predict the effects of media on conversations where there is a "peripheral party."

The concept of tracks is a way of distinguishing between "the official business" of a conversation and talk about the communicative acts by which that business is conducted. When Al says "uh huh" in the conversation described in Table 1, he is not making a contribution to track 1, the business of discussing the repair of the car. He is instead contributing to track 2, talk about the communicative acts that achieve track 1. When Al says "uh huh," he is commenting on Roger's signal that the conversational repair had been successful.

The concept of layers is used to cope with the problem of pretence in fiction, irony teasing, and so on. When I say "There were an Englishman, a Scotsman, and an Irishman standing in a field," you know I am telling a joke. Layer 1 is to pretend layer 2, layer 2 is me proposing the proposition that there were an Englishman... Clark's concepts of tracks and layers have not, to my knowledge, been used to discuss mediated technology. They are included here for completeness.

· · · ·

CHAPTER 5

Case Studies—Applying the Theory to Electronically Mediated Communication

This lecture takes as case studies five published papers that have applied Clark's theory to mediated communication. The theory was developed to explain unmediated face-to-face conversation. As explained in Chapter 4, Clark sees this as the logical starting point for a theory of any kind of language use; indeed, his book's title is *Using Language*. Additional assumptions are needed if the theory is to explain or predict the effects of mediating technology. Each of these case studies builds on Clark's theory to further elaborate it and, in some cases, to make practical suggestions about how different communication media should be used.

5.1   THE COSTS OF GROUNDING (CLARK AND BRENNAN)

A basic principle in Clark's theory, explained in Section 4.1, is that conversants seek to minimize the effort required to communicate and that this is, in a sense, the purpose of developing common ground. Different communication media present different costs to different parts of the grounding process. For example, typing a text message will take more effort than speaking on the phone. However, reading complex instructions from the screen may be easier than having them read to you over the phone. Clark & Brennan (1991) elaborate the theory by analyzing these costs as they apply to different communication media. The extended theory can then be used to explain some of the problems people have with media in particular contexts.

Clark and Brennan characterize the differences between different communication media in terms of which "constraints on grounding" they do and do not provide. In everyday life, "constraints" may be thought to be bad; in this context, they are good as they reduce ambiguity. Take the first constraint copresence. Say we are in the same room and I can see you are looking at a vase of flowers. I can use this common ground to construct a very efficient utterance—"dead, eh?"—to which I might get the expected reply "OK, I'll get rid of them." Had we been conversing on the phone, I would have had to construct quite a long utterance to engage you in the same shared project—"I don't suppose you could possibly chuck out the flowers in the vase on the hall table please?" The phrase "dead eh?" is too ambiguous without the constraints provided by copresence. You might prefer to think of constraints on grounding as "resources for grounding." For the moment, we will stay with Clark and Brennan's terminology.

Clark and Brennan's complete list of constraints on grounding is given in Table 5. Equipment for mediated communication that provided all these constraints would be very good. All these constraints can be viewed as an analysis of the findings from many studies of mediated communication in terms of Clark's theory. The first six of the constraints are advantages of face-to-face

TABLE 5. Clark and Brennan's constraints for grounding
Copresence: A and B share the same physical environment. If I am in the same room as you, I can see and hear what you are doing and I know what you can see and hear and what you are looking at.
Visibility: A and B are visible to one another. If we are video conferencing, I can see you but will not have all the information I would have about you if we were copresent.
Audibility: A and B communicate by speaking. If we are on the phone, I can hear you but will not have all the information I would have about you if we were copresent.
Contemporality: B receives at roughly the same time as A produces. On the phone, you understand what I say at the same time or very soon after I speak. If we are communicating by voicemail, this is not the case.
Simultaneity: A and B can send and receive simultaneously. Face-to-face, I can nod or grunt to show I understand while you are speaking. Other devices may not allow this.
Sequentiality: A's and B's turns cannot get out of sequence. Misunderstandings often arise when e-mails are read in a different order to which they were sent. This is unlikely to be a problem on the phone.
Reviewability: B can review A's messages. Written material can be reread and revisited. Speech fades quickly.
Revisability: A can revise messages for B. E-mails can be read and revised before they are sent. Voice communications have to be repaired in subsequent turns or with extra words in the same turn if trouble is anticipated.

conversation that may be absent in mediated communication. These come from the theory in the sense that mechanisms identified by Clark will not be possible if these constraints are absent. For example, many of the methods of signaling enumerated in Table 3 will not be available without the constraints of copresence and visibility. The tightly coupled process of grounding, described in Section 4.1, will be difficult without audibility, contemporality, simultaneity, and sequentiality. The last two constraints in Table 5 are advantages of written communication identified in studies comparing written and spoken electronic communication.

To predict the problems users may have with a new communication medium, one simply asks which of these constraints are present or absent. The consequence of some medium lacking one or more of the constraints is to increase the costs of some part of the grounding process. For example, if the conversation between the architect Ann and the homeowner Ben developed in Chapter 2 had taken place without the video window, Ben would have had to use words to indicate that he did not understand the word "lintel." This would have been more costly in terms of effort and possible loss of face than looking puzzled. Had they been communicating by writing in a chat window, the cost in effort of signaling, detecting, and repairing this trouble in the conversation is potentially even larger.

People evaluate costs in ways that depend on the purpose of the conversation. Two lawyers communicating about a case may choose the medium of typed letters because it affords the constraints of revisability and reviewability. Here, the cost of an inappropriate joint project being construed by either party is considerable and so the cost of losing all the other constraints is justified. Also, they already have extensive common ground as they are both lawyers who have dealt with this kind of case before. They may choose to meet their clients face-to-face. This is because they need all the constraints they can muster to create some common ground. They know that their view of the case, as a technical problem that must be formulated within a particular legal framework, is quite different from the client's view of the case as a personal problem.

Clark and Brennan's approach was the starting point for a number of papers that use Clark's theory to make predictions about the costs and benefits of using different media for different purposes. Four of these papers that demonstrate the value of their approach are discussed below.

5.2   WHY COGNOTER DID NOT WORK (TATAR, FOSTER, AND BOBROW)

Cognoter was a software tool for use in electronic meeting rooms developed in the 1980s at Xerox PARC as part of the Colab project. The Colab electronic meeting room contained networked computers arranged so that a small group of people could have a meeting together. In a conventional meeting room, people use a whiteboard to coordinate the work. Cognoter was to emulate and enhance the function of a whiteboard through the networked computers and a large-screen central display. The obvious advantages of such a system is that material can be prepared in advance, displayed to the others, changed by the group, and saved for future use. These are all things that are much less easy to do in a conventional meeting room. In addition, Cognoter was designed to facilitate brainstorming by allowing participants to work in parallel. Participants created "items" in an edit window. Items were then displayed to the others on an item organization window as a short catch phrase or title. Anyone could move an item in the item organization window or open it to read and edit the content.

The experiences of users of Cognoter were mixed, and so, Tatar et al. (1991) recruited two groups from outside of the Colab research team to study in detail. Each group consisted of three long-term collaborators who were asked to brainstorm about some subject of their own choosing that would be useful in their work. It was observed that neither group was able to use the item organization window in the way intended. Also, there were numerous conversational breakdowns where Cognoter got in the way of the work they were trying to do. Tatar et al. concluded that the designers of Cognoter had used an inappropriate model of communication, corresponding to the information transfer model depicted in Figure 1. The idea of a Cognoter item as a parcel of information that is constructed and then transmitted to the others may be good for individual brainstorming but simply does not fit in with what happens in the rest of the meeting when discussing what to do with the ideas generated. If one views language use as a closely coupled process of collaborative activity, as depicted in Figure 2, a very different picture emerges. From this perspective, Cognoter items have two functions: as elements in the conversation (signals) and as elements that may be conversed about (common ground). Cognoter did not support either function very well.

When someone is writing on a whiteboard, other participants in the meeting know that they are doing so and can coordinate their actions accordingly. Creating an item with the item editor was a private activity, making this difficult. Also, with a conventional whiteboard, the other participants can see the emerging text as it is written. This allows them to propose modifications and otherwise negotiate and signal common ground as described in Clark's process of grounding. With Cognoter, the author of an item had no idea whether the others had read or even seen it. They could make no assumptions about its status in terms of the level of joint action it was involved in. In terms of Table 4, they could not make any assumptions about levels 1 and 2 in the action ladder. In terms of Clark and Brennan's analysis presented in Section 5.1, Cognotor did not provide the normal grounding constraints expected from copresence, even though all the participants in the meeting were in the same room.

There was a further problem when people tried to refer to items on the item organization window, as the others were likely to be looking at a different version of the display. This was partly due to network delays (an absence of Clark and Brennan's contemporality constraint) but mainly because each display could be scrolled independently. A participant might have scrolled the item organization window so the item another was referring to was not visible. To add to the confusion, the central screen could be displaying a third view onto the item organization window. As was indicated in Section 4.1, pointing is a very effective conversational resource (see Table 3). Pointing may be done with a finger, by voice, or with your eyes (see Section 5.3) and is known in this literature as deixis. Deixis broke down when the person making the reference was looking at a different version of the display from the version the others were looking at. This is another breakdown in the normal grounding constraints provided by copresence. Because of our experience of face-to-face conversation, we expect that, what we can see, everyone else can see too, and so, it is quite difficult to repair these breakdowns.

Tatar et al. suggested some modifications to Cognoter. The features they suggested are now commonly accepted as advantageous with this kind of system and have been implemented in commercial products such as Timbuktu and Netmeeting. They are: (a) fast communication and update of displays; (b) shared editing, where everyone can see the message being composed, letter-by-letter, backspaces and all; and (c) consistent positioning of windows and, if I scroll, so do you. Point (b) comes under the more general design guideline of maximizing "awareness," making everyone aware of what everyone else is doing. Point (c) is an example of the design guideline "what I see is what you see" (WISIWYS). These now widely accepted design principles are given a sound theoretical underpinning by Clark's theory and may even have been, to some extent, inspired by his ideas.

5.3   GAZE AWARENESS: AN EXPERIMENTAL STUDY OF RESOURCES FOR GROUNDING (MONK AND GALE)

The two papers described above exemplify different approaches to the use of Clark's theory. Clark and Brennan took an essentially analytic approach, that is to say, they simply applied the theory to make predictions about how different media might affect communication efficiency. Tatar, Foster, and Bobrow used the theory to analyze some empirical data in the form of detailed transcripts from Cognoter sessions. They applied Clark's theory to these data to describe what went wrong. The analysis was qualitative, providing extracts from these records as evidence for the points made. The study to be described here (Monk & Gale, 2002) took a third approach, which is to make experimental predictions on the basis of the theory and then to provide quantitative evidence for the conclusions drawn.

The resource for grounding examined in this experiment was the ability to judge what someone else is looking at while we are talking. Imagine that we are eating together and I ask you to "pass the jam" and that this statement is ambiguous because there are two pots of jam to choose from. I can tell whether you have correctly guessed that I wanted the strawberry jam before you reach for it simply by monitoring your gaze. If I see you looking at the raspberry jam pot, I can quickly repair the conversation by saying "no, the strawberry please." Most likely, you will draw on the personal common ground we have due to your previous experience of my jam preferences and look at the correct jam pot, thus providing the evidence of understanding that I need. Monk and Gale termed this resource for grounding "full gaze awareness" and contrast it with mutual gaze. Mutual gaze is knowing whether someone is looking at you. Mutual gaze is more commonly known as eye contact and has some well documented functions in regulating conversation and social relationships (Argyle et al., 1974; Goodwin, 1981; Kendon, 1967).

It turns out that both full gaze awareness and mutual gaze are hard to achieve with conventional arrangements for video-mediated communication. Consider the common arrangement of a window showing the head and shoulders of the remote participant via a webcam. The person viewing this image will have their own webcam to transmit a picture of their head and shoulders, which is placed on top to the screen (i.e., above the video image of the remote person). While it may be possible to see whether someone is looking left or right or up or down (Monk and Gale term this partial gaze awareness), there is no possibility for full gaze awareness because none of the objects the remote person may be looking at are visible. To make full gaze awareness possible, a much-wider angle view is required with a scope that includes the person communicating and the objects they are communicating about.

Mutual gaze is made difficult because of the offset between the position of the camera above the screen and the eyes of the remote person on the video image. Mutual gaze has a special place in communication because when I look you in the eye, I know that you know that I did so. If I look you in the eye using the video configuration described above, it will appear that I am looking somewhere on your chest. I can give an illusion of looking you in the eye by looking at the camera but then I cannot monitor the video image to tell if you were simultaneously looking at me.

The problem of achieving mutual gaze can be circumvented using a "video tunnel" (Buxton & Moran, 1990) in which half-silvered mirrors are used to give a camera position which is effectively behind the eyes of the video image of the remote person (see Figure 3). This works in the same way as an autocue, which effectively positions the camera focused on a newsreader a position behind the text he or she is reading. Monk and Gale added a translucent display to this arrangement to provide full gaze awareness. This arrangement, which they call the "GA display" (see Figure 3), was inspired by Ishii's clearboard (Ishii et al., 1993). The translucent display was hung between the participant and the image of the remote person. The illusion to users of the GA display was that the display was positioned between the two participants in the experiment and that they looked through the transparent display to see one another. Although both participants were effectively looking at the

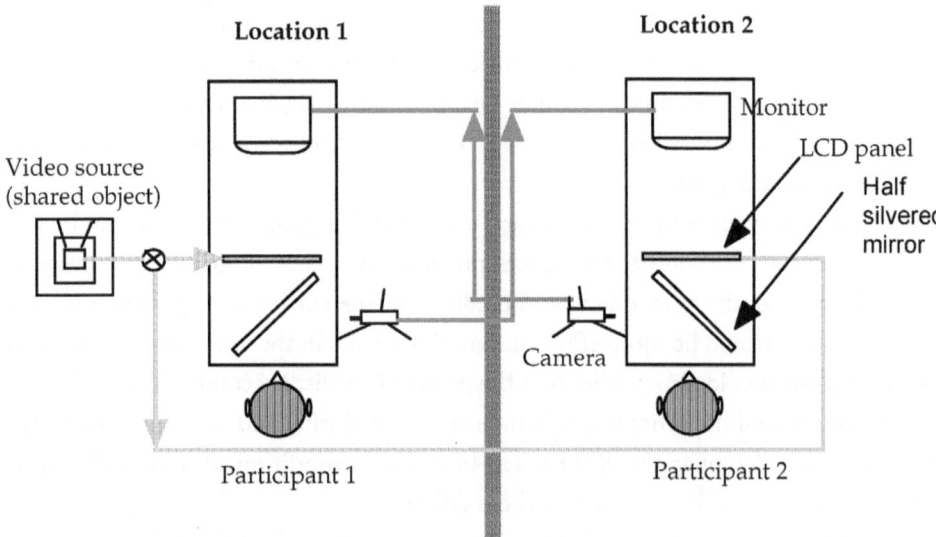

Video feeds to provide image of shared object

Video feeds to provide image of other person

FIGURE 3: The GA display. Each participant sees the other on the video monitor at the end of the video tunnel. A translucent display is hung between the participant and the monitor; the face of the other participant is seen through this display.

same side of this display, that is, they could both read writing on it, there was still full gaze awareness because the mirror left– right transformed the image of the other person apparently behind the translucent display.

The GA display thus provided all the information available to copresent conversational partners but in the context of multimedia communication. The conversational resources of facial expression and mutual gaze were provided by a life-size image of the other person at a distance of 1.5 m. They could establish full gaze awareness through the common image supplied by the spatially separated image on the translucent display at a distance of 0.75 m. The apparatus also made it possible to selectively remove these resources. The experiment compared the GA display with two control conditions, video tunnel only and audio only. The video-tunnel-only condition used half-sized images in different positions on the two translucent displays, thus preventing full gaze awareness. Participants could tell whether the other person was looking up, down, left, or right (partial gaze awareness) but not which element of the display was their current focus of visual attention. In the audio-only condition, the cameras were disconnected so that there was no visual information about the behavior of one's partner.

Eight pairs of participants each used one of these three video configurations. The task required one member of the pair, the "expert," to describe the position of an element in a display. The displays were chosen to be hard to describe, for example, electron microscope images, circuit diagrams, and architectural blueprints. The other member of the pair, the "receiver," had to say which of around 15 labeled points was being described to them. Only one guess was allowed and instructions emphasized that the guess should be correct.

The aim of the experiment was to demonstrate that full gaze awareness could be a resource for grounding above and beyond the resources provided by a view of facial expressions with real mutual gaze. If this was the case, one would predict that the conversations of the pairs using the GA display condition would be more efficient than those pairs in the video-tunnel-only condition. More specifically, one would also predict that the pairs in GA display condition would need to verbally check their own and the other person's understanding of what was said less often than pairs in the control conditions. Comparison of the video-tunnel-only condition with the audio-only condition provided a comparative benchmark for these differences.

To construct a quantitative experiment, notions such as "efficiency" or "checking understanding" have to be quantified in some way (for other examples of how this has been done on experiments looking at common ground, see Convertino et al., 2008; McCarthy et al., 1991). In this experiment,

TABLE 6. Data from Monk and Gale: means and standard deviations for the three video communication configurations

	GA DISPLAY	VIDEO TUNNEL ONLY	AUDIO ONLY
Turns	182 (70)	406 (80)	332 (120)
Words (expert)	1,334 (489)	2,662 (496)	2,111 (883)
Words (receiver)	362 (145)	522 (121)	534 (170)
Checks (your own understanding)	6.12 (4.17)	27.25 (11.4)	17.88 (9.35)
Aligns (the other's understanding)	6.21 (6.19)	19.00 (8.87)	29.62 (16.30)

efficiency was operationalized as the number of turns in the complete session of 20 trials, also as the number of words used by expert and receiver. These are presented in Table 6. There was a large and statistically significant difference between the GA display condition and the control conditions in all three measures (see Monk & Gale, 2002, for details). Pairs using the GA display completed the task in around half the number of turns than those needed in the control conditions. In comparison, there is no statistically significant difference between the two control conditions for any of these measures. Providing a life-size image of the other person's face, with real mutual gaze, had a much smaller and statistically unreliable effect.

The predictions for this experiment were much more specific than just a general improvement in conversational efficiency. Clark's theory predicts that this improved efficiency comes about through differences in the grounding process. Full gaze awareness provides a way checking one's own understanding and that of the other person, so that there should be a reduced incidence of *verbal* checks. To examine this prediction, transcripts were analyzed using a scheme called conversational games analysis (Kowtko et al., 1991; see Monk & Gale, 2002, for details of how it was applied here). In this analysis, checks are sequences of turns in the transcript, initialized by the expert to check the understanding of the receiver. Aligns are similar sequences initialized by the receiver to check their own understanding. Mean counts of these sequences are provided in Table 6. The advantage for the GA display was even more dramatic than observed with the efficiency measures. There were many fewer checks and aligns using the GA display than either control condition. Again, these differences were statistically significant but the difference between the two control conditions was not (see Monk & Gale, 2002, for details).

The contribution of this experiment is to demonstrate that full gaze awareness can be achieved in video-mediated communication, where it can be an important resource for grounding, or "constraint on grounding" in Clark and Brennan's terms. It also provides an example of the opportunities provided by electronically mediated communication for devising experimental manipulations providing interesting tests of the predictions of Clark's theory, something that will be returned to in Section 5.5.

5.4   PREDICTING THE PERIPHERALITY OF PERIPHERAL PARTICIPANTS (MONK)

Watts & Monk (1999) studied general practitioners (GPs) in their treatment rooms communicating over a videophone with medical specialists in a hospital. Figure 4 presents a schematic of this arrangement. The GP was usually in the presence of a patient. There might also be other legitimate overhearers. For example, in one consultation that they observed, the patient was a young girl accompanied by her mother. The consultant was talking to the girl over the video link and asked if she

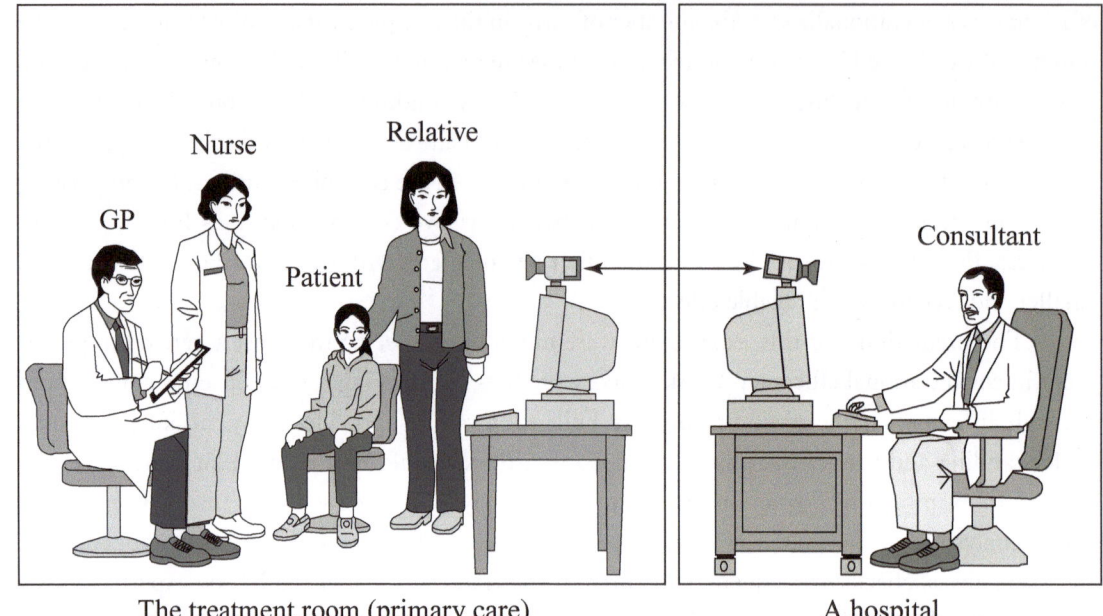

The treatment room (primary care)   A hospital

FIGURE 4: Schematic of the video conferencing context studied by Watts & Monk (1999).

"ate well," to which she replied in the affirmative. The mother disagreed with this and was eventually able to break into the conversation and make this clear.

Watts (1998) characterizes the legitimate overhearers, who are not currently actively involved in the work of the conversation, as peripheral participants. The people currently actively involved in the work are described as primary participants. So, in the above case, the primary participants were the consultant in the hospital and the girl in the treatment room. The mother and the GP were, at that time, peripheral participants. When the mother heard the child indicate that she was a good eater, she felt the need to change her participatory status.

Another example of a legitimate overhearer might be a nurse. Two of the sites that were visited had a nurse who organized the video link and who would generally be present during the consultation. The same nurse might well be involved in treating the patient after the consultation. Having heard the discussion of treatment between GP, patient, and consultant, as a peripheral party, this nurse was in a better position to explain the treatment to the patient. In Clark's terms, the nurse had additional personal common ground due to overhearing.

At all the sites visited, the camera was positioned to give a limited view of the person sitting directly in front of the video link; hence, peripheral participants in the treatment room were unlikely to be visible to the consultant in the hospital. On the basis of Clark's theory, Watts & Monk (1999)

TABLE 7. Participant percept matrix for one instance of telemedical consultation

PERCEPTS	PARTICIPANTS			
	SPECIALIST	GP	PATIENT	NURSE
Specialist's face	–	Yes	Yes	Yes
GP's face	Yes	–	Yes	Yes
Patient's face	No	Yes	–	Yes
Nurse' face	No	Yes	Yes	–
Specialist's voice	–	Yes	No	No
GP's voice	Yes	–	Yes	Yes
Patient's voice	No	Yes	–	Yes
Nurse' voice	No	Yes	Yes	–

The specialist and GP are communicating with telephone handsets and the camera provides the specialist with a limited scope image that only shows the head and shoulders of the GP

formed the hypothesis that, if the specialist in the hospital could not see a peripheral participant, it might make them more peripheral. It might be harder for them to change their participatory status and join the conversation. Also, the primary participants might make fewer allowances for them, in their use of language, for example (see also Section 5.5).

The challenge for Clark's theory then is to predict how a particular audio–video configuration could affect how peripheral a peripheral participant will be. Monk (1999) extends Clark's levels of joint action (Table 4) to do this. The starting point is a participant percept matrix (PPM; Watts & Monk, 1998). This shows who can see and hear what. Table 7 is a PPM for the situation described above. The GP, patient, and nurse are copresent, so they can all see and hear one another. However, because audio is via telephone handsets and the image is of limited scope, not all the percepts are available to all the participants.

Table 8 extends Clark's theory as represented in Table 4 for a two-person conversation to the case of a three-person conversation where C is a close peripheral participant (i.e., someone who is really a part of the conversation but is not the addressee). See Monk (1999) for a full explanation of the term "side participant."

TABLE 8. Levels of joint action with a close peripheral participant (a side participant)

	SPEAKER A'S PART	SIDE PARTICIPANT C'S PART
4	No joint action	No joint action
3	A is signaling that p for B and C	C is recognizing that p from A
2	A is presenting signal s to B and C	C is identifying signal s from A
1	A is executing behavior t for B and C	C is attending to behavior t from A

Table 9 then lists the evidence that might lead A and C to assume that the other is taking part in each level of joint action. There is no joint action at level 4 because C is only a side participant. However, C may feel able to assume they are part of lower-level joint actions. Some of this evidence comes from being able to hear the other person ("H" in Table 9), some from being able to see them ("S" in Table 9). When using this table, one should also recognize Clark's principle of downward evidence in the action ladder. A level 3 joint action is only possible if the corresponding level 1 and 2 joint actions are possible too. This means that evidence that the other person is joining you in a

TABLE 9. Evidence that the other person is taking part in the joint action, speaker and addressee

	EVIDENCE LEADING SPEAKER A TO CONSIDER SIDE PARTICIPANT C	EVIDENCE LEADING SIDE PARTICIPANT C TO CONSIDER SPEAKER A
4	No joint action	No joint action
3	C has responded appropriately to previous signals (H);	A's signal is directed at B and C (H);
	A can hear verbal back channels from C (H);	A's signal refers to common ground specific to C (H)
	A can see visual back channels from C (S)	
2	Only by downward evidence	Only by downward evidence
1	A can see C is attending (S)	C can see A's behavior is directed at B and C (S)

(H) = must be able to hear other; (S) = must be able to see other

level 3 joint action is also evidence that they are joining you in the corresponding level 1 and 2 joint actions.

Table 9 can be used to determine what evidence is available to a primary participant, say the specialist, that would lead them to consider a peripheral participant, say the nurse, to be a side participant, and vice versa. Combining this with an analysis of the evidence available to the other primary participant, the GP, allows an assessment of the overall peripherality of the nurse (i.e., how easy it will be for them to join in the conversation).

The above account shows how Clark's model can be elaborated to make predictions about the effects of small changes to the way a video link is configured. Monk & Watts (2000) present a laboratory experiment where such predictions are made and tested with encouraging results.

5.5   PERIPHERAL PARTICIPANTS IN TEXT CHAT—PUTTING WORDS IN PEOPLE'S MOUTHS (HEALEY AND MILLS)

As was illustrated in Section 5.3, electronically mediated communication provides an opportunity for experimental manipulations that would be difficult or impossible with face-to-face copresent conversation. The experiment described here (Healey & Mills, 2006) is a particularly interesting example of this as it manipulates what was apparently said by automatically adding artificial turns to the conversation as experienced by specific participants. Healey and Mills achieved this by using a text chat conversation as used in instant messaging. Messages, equivalent to turns in speech, are composed and then broadcast to the other participants, where they accumulate in the form of a record of the conversation with turns labeled with the name of the person who sent them (see Figure 5).

Participants worked remotely in pairs to solve a maze task with an "experimenter" as a peripheral participant observing what they were saying and doing. None could see or speak to the others and all communication was by text chat. All messages were relayed through a server. This general-purpose software, that is available free from the authors, performs a linguistic analysis of the messages sent and can subtly change a message before passing it on to the other participants (Healey et al., 2003). Alternatively, as here, artificial turns can be added and attributed to one of the participants. The person who is supposed to have sent the turn does not see it, or any responses to it. Also, the system mimics the speed of typing and spelling (e.g., "txt" conventions) of the person who is supposed to have sent it to make the deception convincing (see Figure 5 for an example).

The theoretical question addressed in this experiment concerns the mechanisms by which primary participants adapt their speech when communicating with a peripheral participant. The maze task was chosen as it had been studied by these investigators in the past. This previous work has provided a detailed description of how pairs of participants adapt the way they describe the maze as the experiment progresses. The final descriptions used are very efficient but require collabo-

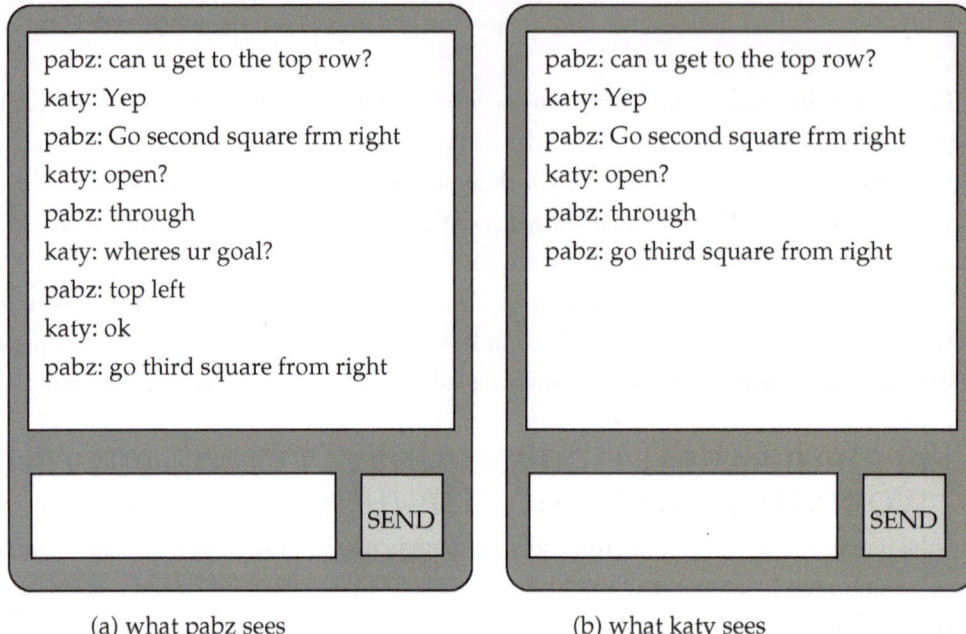

(a) what pabz sees   (b) what katy sees

FIGURE 5: Text chat windows as used by Healey & Mills (2006). The lower box is the turn composition box; text entered there is displayed in the conversation window for both participants when the send button is clicked. Note the three turns beginning "wheres ur goal?" in pabz's window have been inserted by the server as if they had been initiated by katy. For this reason, they are not displayed in katy's window.

ration to establish joint meaning. Clark's theory would predict that primary participants that have achieved this degree of collaboration would assume that a peripheral participant would not have the understanding that they do and, hence, would have to use an earlier, less-efficient description system. This is because, in this experiment, the peripheral participant contributes only briefly at the start of the conversations and takes no part while the collaboration between the primary participants is developing. This means that he is unable to signal that he understands the conversation. An alternative theory (Pickering & Garrod, 2004) predicts that participants respond only to cumulative exposure to linguistic forms, independently of their origin in the conversation.

The server was used to insert questions requiring description of the maze that apparently either came from the other primary participant or the peripheral participant/observer (Figure 5 gives the example of an artificial message apparently coming from the other primary participant). Healey and Mills were then able to analyze the descriptions generated to identical probes sent in similar circumstances in a conversation that seemed entirely natural to the participants.

Thirty-one pairs of participants were recruited as pairs to ensure that they already knew each other. All of them had previous experience of using Internet chat software such as ICQ or Microsoft Messenger. The results supported Clark's theory. The pattern of description types used spontaneously over the experiment changed to become more efficient in the way previously observed. When the responses to the artificially inserted probe questions were analyzed, they followed the same pattern, but only when the apparent originator of the query was the other primary participant. When the originator was apparently the peripheral participant, the pattern of description types was appropriate to the early, less efficient description types, even at the end of the conversation.

Healey and Mills' ingenious experiment demonstrates the radical manipulations that can be made in experiments on communication without sacrificing realism and conversational flow. It also serves to further explore the implications of peripheral participation.

. . . .

CHAPTER 6

Current Status

The five case studies presented above demonstrate that Clark's theory is capable of making useful predictions in the area of electronically mediated communication. Conversely, electronically mediated communication provides interesting possibilities for testing and extending the theory.

In the context of HCI as an engineering discipline, the question then becomes "how realistic is it to apply the theory in a real design context?" At the earliest stages of the application of theory to engineering problems, a theory is only really usable by researchers with a specialist knowledge of the area. At the next stage, application of the theory can be formalized as principles that can be used by a human-factors consultant who has had the time to get to understand the theory and the background material needed. Finally, as the use of the theory matures, it becomes encapsulated as a set of guidelines or rules that can be used directly by a designer with very little background in human factors or human communication.

In an earlier version of this lecture (Monk, 2003), I concluded that the use of Clark's theory was still at the earliest stage and that it was only being used by researchers of language use. I now believe we are moving to the next stage. For example, the theory has been applied to communication between robots and their human operators (Stubbs et al., 2008). The next phase of development will be to gain sufficient practical experience of using the theory in real design contexts to make the shift to a set of well specified guidelines for use in particular contexts: guidelines for configuring multiparty video conferencing, guidelines for desktop video, guidelines for asynchronous communication, and so on. The bandwidth needed for video and voice-based conferencing is now available cheaply via high-speed broadband. Consequently, electronically mediated communication is widely available, making the need for such guidelines increasingly pressing.

The opportunities provided by electronically mediated communication for testing and extending theories of language use were ably illustrated in the case studies presented in Section 5.3 and Section 5.5. As more researchers test the theory and use it to reason about electronically mediated communication, the bounds of the theory and the additional assumptions needed will become apparent. Clark's book is now 12 years old, but it is still the most influential theory of language use when it comes to the practical question of designing communication technology.

· · · ·

CHAPTER 7

Further Reading

Readers interested in the background material (scientific foundations) that Clark's theory draws on should read the tutorial review paper by McCarthy & Monk (1994).

Clark's book (1996) is an accessible and coherent statement of his whole theory. It has useful orienting summaries at the beginning and end of each chapter. Also, the first and last chapters provide accessible summaries of the whole book. He goes to some lengths to explain the scientific foundations of his work. Readers interested in this theory are strongly recommended to buy the book and get it straight from the horse's mouth. Clark & Brennan (1991) is also very accessible.

Other readers may wish to find out more about the research literature on electronically mediated communication. Finn et al. (1997) is a comprehensive set of papers (25 chapters, 570 pages) on video-mediated communication. More generally, see also Balakrishnan et al. (2008), Kraut et al. (2003), Neuwirth et al. (1994), and Vertegaal et al. (2002). The Conference on Human Factors in Computing Systems (CHI), Computer Supported Cooperative Work (CSCW), and European Conference on Computer-Supported Cooperative Work (ECSCW) conferences are also good sources of papers.

. . . .

Acknowledgment

I would like to thank numerous colleagues and students who commented on previous versions of this lecture, particularly Robert Kraut and Patrick Healey.

References

Altmann, G. T. M. (1997). *The ascent of Babel*. Oxford: Oxford University Press.

Argyle, M., Lefebvre, L. M., & Cook, M. (1974). The meaning of five patterns of gaze. *European Journal of Social Psychology, 4*, 125–136.

Balakrishnan, A. D., Fussell, D., & Kiesler, S. (2008). *Do visualisations improve synchronous remote collaboration.* Paper presented at the CHI 2008, Florence Italy.

Buxton, W. A. S., & Moran, T. (1990). EuroPARC's integrated interactive intermedia facility (iiif): early experience. In S. Gibbs & A. A. Verrijn-Stuart (Eds.), *Multi-user interfaces and applications* (pp. 11–34). Amsterdam: Elsevier Science Publishers.

Clark, H. H. (1996). *Using Language*. Cambridge: CUP.

Clark, H. H., & Brennan, S. E. (1991). Grounding in communication. In L. B. Resnick, J. Levine & S. D. Teasley (Eds.), *Perspectives on socially shared cognition* (pp. 127–149). Washington, DC: American Psychological Association.

Convertino, G., Mentis, H. M., Rosson, M. B., Carroll, J. M., Slavkovic, A., & Ganoe, C. H. (2008). *Articulating common ground in cooperative work: content and purpose.* Paper presented at the CHI 2008, Florence, Italy.

Finn, K. E., Sellen, A. J., & Wilbur, S. B. (1997). *Video-mediated communication*. Mahwah, NJ: Lawrence Erlbaum Associates.

Goffman, E. (1976). Replies and responses. *Language in Society, 5*, 257–313.

Goodwin, C. (1981). *Conversational organisation: interaction between speakers and hearers*. New York: Academic.

Grice, H. P. (1957). Meaning. *Philosophical Review, 66*, 377–388.

Healey, P. G. T., & Mills, G. J. (2006). *Participation, Precedence and Co-ordination in Dialogue.* Paper presented at the Cogsci 2006, Vancouver, BC, Canada.

Healey, P. G. T., Purver, M., King, J., Ginzburg, J., & Mills, G. (2003). *Experimenting with Clarification in Dialogue.* Paper presented at the Cogsci 2003, Boston.

Ishii, H., Kobayashi, M., & Grudin, J. (1993). Integration of interpersonal space and shared workspace: clearboard design and experiments. *ACM Transactions on Information Systems, 11*(4), 349–375.

Jefferson, G. (1987). On exposed and enclosed corrections in conversation. In G. Button & J. R. E. Lee (Eds.), *Talk and social organisation*. Clevedon: Multilingual Matters.

Kendon, A. (1967). Some functions of gaze direction in social interaction. *Acta Psychologica, 26*, 22–63.

Kowtko, J. C., Isard, S., & Doherty-Sneddon, G. (1991). Conversational games analaysis in dialogue. In A. Lascarides (Ed.), *Tech. Rep. No. HCRC/RP-26 Publications*. Edinburgh: University of Edinburgh.

Kraut, R. E., Fussell, S. R., & Siegel, J. (2003). Visual information as a conversational resource in collaborative physical tasks. *Human–Computer Interaction, 18*, 13–49.

McCarthy, J. C., & Monk, A. F. (1994). Channels, conversation, cooperation and relevance: All you wanted to know about communication but were afraid to ask. *Collaborative Computing, 1*, 35–60.

McCarthy, J. C., Miles, V. C., & Monk, A. F. (1991). *An experimental study of common ground in text-based communication*. Paper presented at the The ACM CHI'91 Conference on Human Factors in Computing Systems.

Monk, A. F. (1998). Cyclic interaction: a unitary approach to intention, action and the environment. *Cognition, 68*, 95–110.

Monk, A. F. (1999). *Participatory status in electronically mediated collaborative work*. Paper presented at the Proceedings of the American Association for Artificial Intelligence Fall Symposium "Psychological models of communication in collaborative systems," North Falmouth, MA.

Monk, A. F. (2003). Common ground in electronically mediated communication: Clark's theory of language use. In J. M. Carroll (Ed.), *HCI models, theories and frameworks: towards a multidisciplinary science* (pp. 265–289). San Francisco: Morgan Kaufmann.

Monk, A. F., & Gale, C. (2002). A look is worth a thousand words: full gaze awareness in video-mediated conversation. *Discourse Processes, 33*(3), 257–278.

Monk, A. F., & Watts, L. A. (2000). Peripheral participation in video-mediated communication. *International Journal of Human–Computer Studies, 52*(2), 775–960.

Neuwirth, C. M., Chandhok, R., Charney, D., Wojahn, P., & Kim, L. (1994). Distributed Collaborative Writing: A Comparison of Spoken and Written Modalities for Reviewing and Revising Documents. In *Proceedings of ACM CHI'94 Conference on Human Factors in Computing Systems* (Vol. 2, pp. 202). Boston: ACM.

Pickering, M.J. & Garrod, S.C. (2004). Towards a mechanistic psychology of dialogue. *Behavioral and Brain Sciences, 27*, 169–226.

Sacks, H., Schegloff, E. A., & Jefferson, G. (1974). A simplest systematics for the organisation of turn taking in conversation. *Language, 50*(4), 696–735.

Shannon, C. E., & Weaver, N. (1949). *The mathematical theory of communication*. Urbana: University of Illinois Press.

Stubbs, K., Wettergreen, D., & Nourbakhsh, I. (2008). *Using a robot proxy to create common ground in exploration tasks*. Paper presented at the HRI 2008, Amsterdam.

Tatar, D. G., Foster, G., & Bobrow, D. G. (1991). Designing for conversation: lessons from Cognoter. *International Journal of Man–Machine Studies, 34*, 185–209.

Vertegaal, R., Weevers, I., & Sohn, C. (2002). *GAZE-2: an attentive video conferencing system*. Paper presented at the CHI02, Minneapolis.

Watts, L. A. (1998). *Understanding interactive behaviour: a quantitative approach*. Ph D Thesis, University of York, York, UK.

Watts, L. A., & Monk, A. F. (1998). Reasoning about tasks, activities and technology to support collaboration. *Ergonomics, 41*(11), 1583–1606.

Watts, L. A., & Monk, A. F. (1999). Telemedicine: what happens in teleconsultation. *International Journal of Technology Assessment in Health Care, 15*(1), 220–235.

Author Biography

Andrew Monk is professor of psychology at York University. His current research is in all areas of technology for the home. He has a long history in usability research, particularly lightweight methods for use by designers and videoconferencing. He is director of the Center for Usable Home Technology (CUHTec) and a fellow of the British Computer Society.